The Seasons

Poetry of the Heart

Poetry of the Heart

KERI MCLEROY

The Seasons
Poetry of the Heart
Copyright © 2020 by Keri McLeroy

Library of Congress Control Number: *2020903047*
ISBN-13:   Paperback: *978-1-64749-057-7*

Poetry

All rights reserved. No part of this publication may be reproduced, distributed, or transmitted in any form or by any means, including photocopying, recording, or other electronic or mechanical methods, without the prior written permission of the publisher or author, except in the case of brief quotations embodied in critical reviews and certain other noncommercial uses permitted by copyright law.

Although every precaution has been taken to verify the accuracy of the information contained herein, the author and publisher assume no responsibility for any errors or omissions. No liability is assumed for damages that may result from the use of information contained within.

Printed in the United States of America

GoToPublish LLC
1-888-337-1724
www.gotopublish.com
info@gotopublish.com

I want to dedicate this to the friends and family who told me to go through with publishing. But I wouldn't be here without my Heavenly Father who gave me the ability of creativity; and my parents, Wayne and Michelle McLeroy for always having my back and encouraging me to go for everything I want to do with my life. I also want to make it known that if it wasn't for my just as talented with writing grandmother, Judy Mathis, I would have never had this capability.

Contents

1	I Have Everything but You (2001)	1
2	Lord (2003)	2
3	Life (2008)	2
4	Love (2009)	3
5	Protect Me (2009)	3
6	Friends Forever (2009)	4
7	Love Is... (2010)	4
8	What is Love? (2010)	5
9	My Heart is Yours (2010)	5
10	Moon (2013)	6
11	If Only You Knew (2013)	7
12	Even From a Far (2013)	7
13	Within All (2013)	8
14	Truest Friends (2013)	8
15	Madness (2013)	9
16	Untitled (2013)	9
17	You and I (2013)	10
18	Patience Equals Love (2013)	10
19	To Mend a Broken Heart (2013)	11
20	Kindest Heart (2011)	11
21	My Love for You (2011)	12
22	Night Skies (2015)	13
23	Summer Love (2015)	14
24	You're Still the One I Want (2015)	15
25	Open (2015)	15

26	There once was a time (2016)	16
27	She Tries (2016)	16
28	Love and Life (2016)	17
29	An End (2016)	18
30	Thoughts (2016)	18
31	Where Did the Time Go? (2013)	19
32	Smile (2013)	19
33	I Seen You Today (2016)	20
34	She Knows (2016)	21
35	Believe (2017)	22
36	You are Where I Belong (2017)	23
37	Siren (2018)	24
38	Dearest (2018)	24
39	Look into the Mirror (2018)	25
40	The Rose (2018)	25
41	Momma's Lullaby (2018)	26
42	Star-Crossed Lovers (2019)	26
43	Always with you (2019)	27
44	Natural Attraction (2019)	28
45	I Salute (2019)	28
46	Daddy's Girl (2019)	29
47	A Mother's World (2019)	29
48	Strength to Surpass (2019)	30

I Have Everything but You

When I look up, I see your face

But you are always with somebody else, you just can't look at me

And now I have everything but you I wish I had you I wish I did

I have everything but you, you are all I ever need

But when you look at me I can't look at you, it just can't be

And now I have everything but you I wish I had you I wish I did

I have everything but you, you are all I ever need

How are we supposed to do this? What are we supposed to do? How are we going to make it to us?

And now I have everything but you I wish I had you I wish I did

I have everything but you, you are all I ever need

Lord

When I look up in the sky, I see you Lord

When I look in the water I see you Lord

When I look beside me, I see you Lord

Lord, you are all I need to keep me alive

Lord, when I need someone to talk to you are always there for me

Lord, you are king

When I need someone to care for me you are always there for me

When I don't feel love and faith, you are always there to bring me back

Lord, you are all I need to keep me alive

Lord, when I need someone to talk to you are always there for me

Lord, you are king

Life

Life is just a memory of events that will eventually be lost...

You will always have friends that you will lose at some point...

Then you will have friends that will just go their separate ways...

So either way people lose at it...

Some people never find true love...

When others do but they don't realize it until they lose them...

So it's a good idea to pay attention to your life...

Instead of just not paying any attention...

Who knows you might just find the right person or find out what you should do with your life

Love

You are the key to my heart

The sun in my sky

The light in my darkness

You are my everything

I love you so much forever and always

Protect Me

Protect me my love, for thy are my guardian angel

Protect me my love, from the treacherous darkness of the night

Protect me my love, wrap thy arms around me for they are my safety

Protect me my love, for your love is the security I'll always need

Protect me my love

Friends Forever

We're always there for one another

When you cry, I cry

When you're sad, I'm sad

When you're happy, I'm happy

When you need help, I say "what's the problem?"

When you need a place to stay, I say "I'm on my way"

We're friends forever

You're my best friend forever & always no matter what

Love Is…

Love is precious

Love is pure

Love is true

Love is when you're around the one who has your heart

Love is when you're constantly thinking about your significant other

Love is a part of life

Love is beautiful

What is Love?

What is love?

Is it ever true?

Is it ever real?

If love is true and real then where is it and why does it end in pain?

Love is a dream for that is the only place it ever actually ends in happiness

My Heart is Yours

I love you with all of my heart!

You're always on my mind, day and night!

I long for your touch!

You always have me knowing I'm safe when I'm in your loving arms!

You're sweet, caring, loving, funny, just absolutely amazing!

Thank you for everything you do, never change!

I love you just the way you are!

I'm yours, forever and always!

Moon

Moon oh moon you shine so bright oh what florescent light you have tonight

Moon oh moon you shine so bright oh how beautiful you are tonight

If Only You Knew

If only you knew what you mean to me

If only you knew what your touch does to me

If only you knew all the things I see in your eyes

If only you knew how much faith I have in you

If only you knew how much I love you

If only you knew

Even From a Far

We've been there for one another for as long as I can remember

Laughed together, cried together

Heck we've been through it all together

But no matter what we've got each other's back

We're as close as sisters if not closer

As well as the best of friends even from a far

Within All

The darkest of nights, the brightest of days shall never cease

The wind of the night is still the wind of the day

As to I am dark, you are light

Where shall we meet?

We live in one of the same

Truest Friends

The truest of friends are there till the end

They watch out for you when times are rough

They are there for you when you need someone to talk to

Get in trouble, if they're not right beside you, they'll get you out

Near or far it doesn't matter the distance, the truest of friends have no distance

They'll always be there in the end

Madness

Have I gone mad?

What is going on, do you hear that sound?

It sounds like drums but wait there are voices to, huh?

Someone please help me, oh I don't hear anything anymore

Where did it all go?

Wait a second it was all in my head

Hmmm… maybe I have gone mad!

Untitled

Smile because that's all you know how to do

Try your best to hide your thoughts and hide feelings

Be there for the people you care about because that's what you've always done

Don't worry about yourself til you're all alone

Worry because it doesn't seem possible to do other wise

Constantly have stuff on your mind and can never seem to lose them

Just try your best to live day by day!

You and I

You warm my heart, like the sun warms the earth

You give me joy, like children at play

When you're around me, I'm vulnerable and weak

But when you're nowhere near I'm cold as can be

You brighten my days, and your arms are my shield at night

I lay my head upon your chest, while listening to your heart I peacefully rest

Patience Equals Love

Be patient don't rush

The right time will come

Patience equals love

Love equals a life time companion

A life time companion equals eternity

Eternity means love will never end

To Mend a Broken Heart

Cover up your pain with a smile

Cover up your heart with a wall

Don't allow love till you know you've recovered

Or maybe you should allow it and you will recover

Because the last thing you want to do is be alone forever

Kindest Heart

He is strong, caring, and kind

A hard worker and is always there for his family and friends

He has the sweetest smile and eyes that will read right through you

He listens to all problems and helps if he can

He has the kindest heart I've ever seen

My Love for You

My love for you is like a rose it shows passion, beauty, strength, and patience!

I love you with all my heart and soul!

Night Skies

Night Skies are beautiful, country or city, you can always find comfort looking at the moon and stars

Summer Love

Summer days and summer nights

Love and lust is in the air, it may go all summer long but will it last through winter spring and fall

You're Still the One I Want

I can't seem to get you out of my head and I can't seem to take my heart back from you

It doesn't seem to matter what is going on or how confusing things have gotten

You are the only one I want to lay my head beside and you have the only arms I want to feel wrapped around me when I sleep

You're still the one I want

Open

Open your eyes to see a new day

Open your heart to let God's hands in

And open your soul to do his will

Open your mind to God's word

Open your eyes to see a new day

There once was a time

There once was a time that you could feel passion between us

There once was a time that I seen nothing but love in your eyes

There once was a time that sex felt like making love

There once was a time but where is that time now

Yes we have had our problems but somehow we got through it though as time goes on and on it all goes back to there once was a time

She Tries

On the outside you don't see what she puts herself through

She knows she hurts you but she hurts herself as well

She tries not to fight but causes them by trying to please you but also trying to be true to herself

She doesn't know what to do or how to talk on the matter because it worries her

She cares for you but she cares for people that you don't like as well

She tries to make some sort of a compromise by keeping her distance from these friends but it still doesn't work

Love and Life

To love you is something I cannot explain

To ignore you is impossible

We are only friends I know and yet it kills me inside

I would give up my life for you but would you for mine?

I'm sorry for all my wrong doings & I'm trying to just be a friend because I know that is what you want of me at least for the time being but I've always had a stronger sense with you than I have ever had. I've tried and tried and tried to ignore my feelings for you but even if I can kick them for a little while they seem to kick me right back and my worry for you doesn't help me any but I'm going to control myself for the best I can because I don't know what I'd do if I were to actually lose you so here is my promise to you. I will always stand by you and be there for you and give my opinion when you want it. And just be your friend unless someday you actually decide to give me an actual chance. Though I can't wait forever. Just know I will always love you and be there for you.

An End

Do you ever feel like what you have has come to an end?

Like when there was a fire between you but now it's just ashes

What has changed have you grown apart?

Will the flame come back to life or will the ashes be swept away by the wind?

That's the funny thing about love you never know where it will take you.

Your fire can be a passionate flame at first, which sometimes it will remain

Or it can casually cease into ashes and send you in a new direction

So do you ever feel like what you have has come to an end?

Thoughts

I thought I hid my feelings far away

I thought I could keep it from showing

I thought I could manage without you

But I thought wrong

The feelings remain they show unexpectedly and tear me apart inside

I will always love you and that will never change

But I have to seal away my feelings for you

Because it's what best to do

Maybe someday I won't have to hide them anymore

Where Did the Time Go?

Where did the time go?

Where did things go wrong?

We use to be so close but now we're so far apart

I was always your little girl, I still am

I see you more and more in me each and every day and all I see is a lost daughter wondering what has happened to her father

Smile

The more I'm with you the more I'm smiling

When I think of you the more I'm smiling

When you wrap your arms around me the more I'm smiling

Trust me honey I could go on and on about how you keep me this way but I'll just sum it up with this

All I know is that I'm grateful for you being in my life and for keeping this smile on my face.

I Seen You Today

I seen you today and at first I was happy

I seen you today and than I seen her

I seen you today and at first my heart was melting

I seen you today and than due to her it shattered

I seen you today and I realized I can't let you matter

I seen you today and I realized I can't keep you from mattering

I want you happy because no matter how much I care for you I'm with him

No matter how much I miss you I have to let you go

No matter how much I love you I chose him

I'll always be there for you even when I'm not present

I seen you today

She Knows

She knows of all the pain she has done to you

She knows but she can't take it back

She tries to move forward with you

But the past keeps coming back

You say we'll move forward

But do you really think that's possible?

How can it be when you don't let go of the wrong done?

You say she doesn't try for you

You say that she's always in the wrong

But have you even tried to see her side?

Do you see what your choice of ill words causes her on some nights?

You say you love her and want her for eternity

But yet did you ever notice that the past that doesn't disappear is what keeps the cycle going?

She knows she's done you wrong but without the past there is no future, and without learning to forgive and trust again

The relationship is over

Believe

Sing me a song of love and harmony

Sing me a song of hope and dreams

Brighten my darkness because you are the light in me

Hold me near as I'm afraid to fall

For falling leads to pain, and pain leads to despair

For all the pain, I've done to you

You still believe in us

You are Where I Belong

It's that wrap me up and never let me go

It's feeling at peace walking through the door

It's the smile that runs across your face

And the look in your eyes

It's knowing no matter what you'll be by my side

It's a once in a lifetime kind of feeling

It's everything a girl ever dreams of

For you, my heart wonders

And for you, I feel at home

I can feel that it's true

You are where I belong

*1 Corinthians 13:4-8 "Love suffers long *and* is kind; love does not envy; love does not parade itself, is not puffed up; does not behave rudely, does not seek its own, is not provoked, thinks no evil; does not rejoice in iniquity, but rejoices in the truth; bears all things, believes all things, hopes all things, endures all things. Love never fails. But whether *there are* prophecies, they will fail; whether *there are* tongues, they will cease; whether *there is* knowledge, it will vanish away."*

Siren

She has a way about her

Sweet as can be

Eyes that make you wonder

And lips that cause "O"

Natural at head turns

Though she never notices

She ponders on the idea

As hearts keep falling

Without a doubt

She is a Siren

Dearest

Why didn't you fight harder? Did you think you lost me due to what you did to me? You have always had me even when we're apart, regardless on what life brings. What happened needed to happen even though things was good, your eyes needed to be opened up so there wouldn't be a problem later. Protection will always be done. Regardless of what the outcome brings me. Though I like that I put things at a high standard for you because it makes it where I know I did my best.

Look into the Mirror

Look into the mirror and tell me what you see

Is it independence or dependence?

Is it beautiful or ugly?

Is it strong or weak?

Is it happy or sad?

Every emotion is there but only you can fight

No one can change it without you giving to the change

Look into the mirror for the truth in you to be seen

The Rose

It has its thorns

It has its beauty

It can bring on a smile

Or it can cause you pain

For whichever it might be

Is yours to choose

For I am the rose

Momma's Lullaby

Near nor far you are on my mind

Light or dark your smile brings joy

Heaven nor hell knows the depths of a mother's love

For you are like no other and I am proud to call you mine

Star-Crossed Lovers

Two hearts beating as one

A profounding love for one another

You take my breath away but yet you give me life

You are Marc Anthony to my Cleopatra

A touch like no other

Just a kiss to truth

We know our love is true

Just like star-crossed lovers

Always with you

Just because you can no longer hear me does not mean that I cannot hear you

Just because you can no longer hold me does not mean I am not holding you

Just because you can no longer see me does not mean I am not watching you

No matter where you are and no matter what you do I am always with you

Near or far, look inside your heart and you will see that I am still there

Live and be happy we will be together again one day

A poem from a loved one

*John 17:24 "Father, I desire that they also whom You gave Me may be with Me where I am, that they may behold My glory which You have given Me; for You Loved Me before the foundation of the world."

Natural Attraction

What is it about us?

This tension between us has been here since the day we laid eyes on each other

My breath ceases when your lips touch mine

Our hearts carry the same beat as you pull me closer

Neither really have to do a thing to be excited about the other

It's a natural attraction between you and I

At first you fought this feeling

And now I'm fighting this feeling

Pull me closer so the pain of ignorance disappears

Don't let me fight this feeling anymore

Lay your lips on mine once more

So I remember this natural attraction once again

I Salute

I salute the brave

The ones who fight so we can be free

I salute the wounded

The ones who given their lives for you and me

I salute thee

Daddy's Girl

Small enough to fit in the palm of your hand

Though you was terrified due to my size

You held me in the air playfully

I was your little shadow, following you where I could

We may have our ups and downs

But you are my father and I am your daughter

For no matter what

I will always be a daddy's girl

A Mother's World

They care for you from the very beginning

They make sure you are their first priority

They cloth you, feed you, and shelter you

They teach you discipline, love and compassion

They want the best for you

No matter what you do

In the eye of a mother

You're their world!

Strength to Surpass

Lost and confused

Dreams are now broken

I'm only 15 now what will I do?

Ignore and ignorance

It'll stop happening soon

Dislocation after dislocation

Okay maybe I should be aware

Read and study

Don't be afraid of what will happen

Strong beautiful no matter the outcome

Fight the invisible and unseen

Because this disease will be your downfall

But only if you allow it to be

*God never puts something on us that we can't pull through. With any test, he gives us strength to surpass it. This is for anyone with a health issue visible or invisible, it doesn't matter!

www.ingramcontent.com/pod-product-compliance
Lightning Source LLC
LaVergne TN
LVHW070046070526
838200LV00028B/408